Faith
(RE)CONSTRUCTION

———————•———————

31 Day Journey
Deconstructing Your Faith
Without Losing It

GEOFF THIESSEN

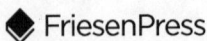

◆ FriesenPress

Suite 300 - 990 Fort St
Victoria, BC, V8V 3K2
Canada

www.friesenpress.com

ISBN
978-1-5255-7441-2 (Hardcover)
978-1-5255-7442-9 (Paperback)
978-1-5255-7443-6 (eBook)

1. RELIGION, CHRISTIAN LIFE, SPIRITUAL GROWTH

Distributed to the trade by The Ingram Book Company

Dedication

———•———

I am dedicating this book to Dennis Willows,
a dear friend who passed far too soon.
Thank you for your dedicated support
and ongoing encouragement to tackle
this project. You are greatly missed.

Introduction

———•———•———

In my early years and into my adulthood, I, like so many others, struggled with my faith as I tried to understand where God fit in and how it ought to reflect in my everyday life. I had many questions but few answers, and my quest was to find more than what I was being taught. This led me on an incredible life-changing journey of faith. I don't see myself as a writer, yet I do realize I have something to say. Perhaps my journey of faith will inspire you on yours. I've come to learn that freedom is powerful and that understanding God—not religion—can transform the very foundation of our life. I've learned that God is never afraid of our questions, disappointments, or struggles with our beliefs, and that life is a journey. Following Jesus is a life-long experience that can't be put into a neatly squared off box. Faith is alive, always growing, and ever-changing.

It's with this personal journey in mind that I was encouraged to sit down and pen some of my experiences and thoughts on how my faith shifted and my relationship with Jesus redefined me as a person. Like you, I am a real person, serving a real Jesus with a passion to see people experience real, unmanufactured and system-less faith. My faith wasn't real but a carbon copy of what I'd been taught and told to experience. In the next thirty-one days, you'll see struggle, frustration, unlearning, and incredible transformation.

This project was many months in the making, with lots of early morning sit downs at the same table at my favourite Tim Hortons. With a freshly brewed cup of coffee and sometimes a muffin, a Bible and iPhone, it all began. This thirty-one-day journey will inspire hope, challenge the status quo, and invite you to an authentic faith experience.

I've learned that following Jesus is much more than a well-packaged set of beliefs. It's not denominational, nor is it about a set of rules to follow that when you don't get it —you're out. I have found faith to be exciting, and it completely fits into everyday, "normal" life. It's never about living ideals but about making changes as we look into His Word and interact and journey with its truth. For so long I sat faithfully in those pews, wondering why I didn't fit in, why I couldn't just toe the line, why I struggled with what I was seeing and often hearing. Something was missing. I was trying to make sense of things but coming away feeling like I'd just simply failed.

I'm excited that you're on this journey with me, and I hope that as you're reading, you'll look differently at faith and some of the things you've been taught. It's my intent for you to have "a-ha" moments that lead to freedom and authenticity in your journey of faith. I want you to discover the personal-ness of Jesus and that His life and words are exactly what's needed to make the most of your everyday experiences. You will see that He's never about pointing a finger but lending a hand, never about conformity but authenticity, and never the author of confusion.

You will see that Jesus speaks life, believes the best of you, is always there for you, and is committed to seeing you through whatever stands in front of you. For these next thirty-one days, come along with me. It will be fun, interactive, challenging, eye opening, encouraging, empowering, and life changing!

Make your faith real and genuinely yours; don't copy others. Your life and walk of faith with Jesus awaits you.

Day 1

IS YOUR
FAITH BEING TESTED?

I was always led to believe that God would "test" our faith to see if it's real or genuine (as if He doesn't know that already). It even sounded biblical—after all, the best way to show that you were a "true" follower of Jesus was by your commitment, or as I'd like to put it, "performance." It didn't take long to learn this art (I had bumps along the way). Often, I would "commit" myself with even greater purpose to perform better. This went on for years! As a result, I built a false sense of what it meant to be a follower of Jesus. Hey, I didn't smoke, drink, swear, or listen to rock music. I went to church and looked down on people who, well … did all those things. My righteousness was purely self-generated, but somehow, I managed to give God all the credit. I would study the Bible and learn or develop what I thought were perfect doctrines. And wow! I believed I had things exactly where they needed to be. Testing of my faith? Bring it on! I was ready, committed, and wanted an opportunity to show the world.

As I grew older and experienced disappointment after disappointment, frustration, and a sense of walking/running on a hamster wheel of a largely self-produced Christianity, I started to look at testing not as proving or showing off my faith but as pointing out where I wasn't making it. I had come to learn that that's what God does (**not true**). I thought God pointed out our failures, shortfalls, and doctrinal issues so that we'd know where we needed to rely on Him to change. That produced in me a distaste and dislike for God, because I felt like a failure. I believed that God, through these testings, would prove this not only for me, but for everyone around me, to see.

The church culture I grew up in was a giant mirror, or finger-pointing agency, exposing failure. Bible verses were used to further solidify that point. Preaching was often focused on our sin, failures, and shortcomings. I look back now and realize that people meant well, but I think it was also a decoy to hide their "own stuff" and make themselves look good. The more you focus on other people's testings, the less attention your own attract.

Long story short—I have come to understand some transformational truth that has set the course of my life and how my *Father* (not boss) views the testing of my faith. The testing is to prove to us His truth and to demonstrate that His performance is completely adequate. I simply need to let His life take root, and He lives it through me! I have learned that relationship is the heart of everything Jesus demonstrated! He isn't about exposing sin, failure, and shortcomings but rather revealing to us who we really are and what He has given us. His truth and life in us **never** fails—that's why the testing of our faith in the book of James guarantees that it will reveal His powerful fruit in us. He's going to test it right before our very eyes for us to see and witness. To add to that powerful truth, James says, "Consider it pure joy, my brothers and sisters, whenever you face trials of many kinds, because you know that the testing of your faith produces perseverance" (James 1:2–3, NIV). God will do this all the time, anywhere, no matter what!

POWER THOUGHT:
It's not about doing more but letting what God has already done come *alive* in you.

PERSONAL REFLECTION: What is your faith producing and what do others see?

Day 2

WHEN CHRISTIANITY POSES A PROBLEM

find it very hard to hold back when I'm really bothered by something. Sometimes in the swing of emotions, my filters can be challenged. But hey, sometimes shock and awe brings needed change! And yes … I know it needs to be the right kind of shock and awe. Growing up in a church culture, I usually learned the hard way. I was never a toe-the-line type of person, and I learned over the years that reformer-types never are. They bring change, challenge the system, push boundaries, and question the things that seem to accomplish nothing. Needless to say, this can cause unintended conflict where conformity is expected.

People are all different, and too often we let those differences divide us instead of making us stronger. We tend to highlight and focus on those differences. Jesus taught so much about working together, being unified, and not comparing ourselves to others. Many people in my life are different than me—they believe differently and have different values, interests, ways of expressing themselves, and hobbies. They're different but they're not projects for me to change. Every person in my life, whether for the short term or the long term, has contributed something to make me who I am. God has given a piece of Himself to each one, and I choose to celebrate that.

Do I get along with everyone? Not a chance! Some people irritate me, push my buttons, and on occasion make me … well … you know! Such is life. Growing up in a church culture, I was taught that everyone is important and equal in God's sight, yet sometimes we practiced the very opposite. (I think that still plagues certain dynamics of the church.) That's where Christianity can pose a problem (notice I didn't say God, but Christianity). The more I learn and grow in my walk with Jesus, the more I see people differently. I purpose to remove labels, and I don't expect people to believe the way I do. I give them the grace and the room needed for them to walk out their own journey.

People are the most valuable assets we can ever have in life, and we do them and ourselves an injustice when our belief system or theology excludes and labels them. Jesus designed and intended the church to bring life and kingdom impact! If we make that the true heart issue, our doctrine and theology (which are important) will never be divisive. Real heart Christianity says that everyone matters, and everyone is important; it will always be seen and demonstrated through our actions. I get so encouraged when I read about how Jesus treated and interacted with people who were different than Him. I don't waste time debating theology or what is "pure doctrine." Nope, I occupy my time learning to value people and make it my intention to be like Jesus everywhere I go.

POWER THOUGHT:
Our faith should never create barriers but birth possibilities.

PERSONAL REFLECTION: How have labels affected your interactions with people around you?

Day 3

WHAT REALLY MATTERS?

Sometimes I feel a bit apprehensive about writing down my thoughts because of potential backlash or misunderstanding. Growing up in the church culture, it was easy to fall out of good standing for not toeing the line or for questioning certain doctrines of the faith. But as I get older, I'm developing more of an I-don't-care mentality—not because I'm mad or upset, but because I'm tired of the uselessness of it.

Doctrine and theology have a place, but too often it's at the expense of relationships and evangelistic efforts. We forget that it's people we're seeing and talking to, not projects. We can be so busy making sure we have the correct theology that we miss the real reason we're here in the first place.

I didn't have a good experience with church culture, so as a pastor, I keep that in mind. Using the Bible to point out wrong or failure does the opposite of what Jesus demonstrated. So what really matters? This is the million-dollar question, because when we get this, we'll unlock the key to impacting people with powerful, measurable results.

Every church defines this question differently, but the proof or measuring stick is in the impact it leaves in the community outside of the four walls of our buildings. For so long the church has prided itself in its programs, conferences, prayer summits, or worship culture, but with no measurable impact outside the walls. We get excited about the feelings, encounters, and even breakthroughs, but if it's not measurable outside the walls, what does it really matter?

Wherever Jesus walked, He left an impact. He disrupted the religious system and burst the security bubbles of the religious, transforming people and the community. I wonder at times what we're so afraid of. Society is tired of hearing what the church is against and what it wants changed. Our voice no longer has any value or relevance! And I totally understand! So let's change that—not by a new program or event, or a resurgence of doctrine, but by getting hold of what really matters and loving and caring for people by being Jesus in everyday life.

POWER THOUGHT:
Our worldview must become bigger than ourselves.

PERSONAL REFLECTION: What are some ways that you can positively shape your worldview?

Day 4

TO AGREE OR NOT AGREE

know this is a distorted rendition of one of Shakespeare's famous lines, but I think it's a good one to consider when it comes to church or Christianity. Let me be clear—I'm not against church. I'm a pastor of a church; I believe in the church. I happen to believe that when we understand our role, the church can be the most powerful organism in the world. I just struggle with how it's so often represented. I think it often misses God's intended purpose.

Church should not be a gathering place just for the saints, or what we so easily call "the saved," but a place for the public, for our community, to encounter the kingdom. Our signs say "All welcome," but are all welcome? Think about it just for a minute: "All welcome," yet we tend more often than not to require everyone to think like us, believe like us, sing like us, and hold to our particular values (theology). Is it possible to be spiritual, love Jesus, and differ with any of the above? I guess the proof is in the pudding! We may not agree with our particular culture, the choices or lifestyles people embrace, and we may not agree with where the community is heading or what new trends are hitting the main stage, but is it about agreeing or not agreeing?

Jesus was never a lifestyle crusader, nor was He the theology police. Wherever Jesus went and spent time with people, life was birthed, freedom came, and hope was encountered. The only people He confronted were the religious ones, and He didn't mince words with them.

It's not about agreeing or disagreeing with what's happening around us—it's about loving, serving, and manifesting Jesus! We need to stop making it about us, our brand of Christianity, and how the world needs to come into alignment with us. We need to make it about Jesus and manifesting *Him* to the people/community around us! Only then will we see the community impacted, self-righteousness disintegrated, and true kingdom transformation.

POWER THOUGHT:

Differences should never divide us ... they should only make us stronger

PERSONAL REFLECTION: What are some ways that differences can make you stronger?

Day 5

ARE WE ASKING
THE RIGHT QUESTIONS?

It's often easy to write someone off based on their actions or choices. We just have to listen to the news, drive in traffic, get into a debate, or participate in a congregational meeting at church to see how natural it is for people to get their dander up in a roar! I used to find it quite amusing (congregational meetings, that is) when I was young, but now it just irritates me to no end. It usually concerns a doctrinal or theological issue, or our rendition of "biblical truth," and not the need to have a heart for people and impact our community.

People are often unengaged or uninterested in church altogether (even those who grew up in it or have been part of some religious affiliation). It's interesting to see how the church responds to this. Often we make assumptions and poke at the shallowness of people's commitment to their faith, or their lack of resolve. I think we can make a lot of assumptions and come up with a variety of conclusions but I wonder if we care enough to ask the right kind of questions.

Could it be that some of our belief systems have segregated people, forced them into certain camps, and created pressure to perform a certain way? And let's not forget expectations—this is a big one! Let's be real—no one wants to disappoint. Jesus demonstrated the exact opposite and HE IS perfect theology...sometimes ours just plugs us up.

Just thinking out loud ... are people tired of the religious system, or putting on a polished front that doesn't allow them to think outside the box or be creative? Perhaps they're struggling with some of the things they were taught—or worse yet, they've been labeled for not toeing the traditional line. I'm not being negative … just wondering. Are people tired of the fake and just want the real? Tired of not being heard as they struggle for answers?

I believe the church has created overwhelming casualties in the name of the system, doctrine, and its teaching of Bible truth. Hey, I'm not suggesting that we open the floodgates, or that nothing matters and doctrine is meaningless; however, we need to address our attitude, practice, and interactions with people. Jesus always was about people, and He asked the right questions. In turn, they encountered life-changing —transformational truth!

Jesus was *not* known for truth (although He is the truth). He *wasn't* known for His theology (although He is perfect theology). He *was known* for his impact on people, communities, and the world. So let's ask the right questions, because how we care about people and their journeys is what really matters!

POWER THOUGHT:

Asking the right questions will always help find the right solutions.

PERSONAL REFLECTION: How can asking the right questions help in your situations?

Day 6

WHAT'S IN A NAME?

We all have a name. Some of us have 'many' of them. Each of those names usually expresses something about us or the person we are communicating with. Some we laugh about, and others we don't care for (especially if they point to one of our negative habits or apparent flaws). These names often turn into labels.

When we label or view people a certain way, we tend to treat them differently, justifying our actions in the process. In a world where people are trying to find who they are, it's easy to label them, especially if they don't fit into our particular belief system. This is where we can do incredible damage. Jesus made room for people to process, make their journey, and question things without making them feel excluded or condemned.

I believe that our belief system ought never to segregate people, nor should it produce an "us and them" mentality. Jesus was inclusive, engaging, and completely passionate about people and their journeys. He always met them where they were and always spoke to their potential and value. Words are powerful, and when they're used correctly, they transform people and explode the kingdom in them!

When we see people who are different than us, we must look carefully at what we see, because this will translate into how we treat them. We need a real honesty to come over the church. We don't have it altogether, nor is our theology or doctrine as perfect as we'd like to think. We too are in process and on a journey, and to act as though we've arrived sends the wrong message.

If we're to be effective and make a tangible difference in our communities and world, it won't be from Bible verse wars or pointing fingers at those who need to "get it." (Who would want to in the first place?) And it won't be through our doctrinal positions, which too often come across as heartless and demeaning. No, it will be through the way we value and treat them. Perhaps the verse that speaks to this clearly is Matthew 7:12a: "So in everything, do to others what you would have them do to you…" Simple but powerful! We need to see people as people, and until we learn to do that, it's best to keep our evangelism strategy, witnessing techniques, and even our great knowledge of the Bible in a locked closet somewhere. We need to learn the art of valuing and caring for people without labels, pretenses, or personal agendas.

POWER THOUGHT:

How we view people is directly related to how we treat them.

PERSONAL REFLECTION: How can you change how you view or value the people around you?

Day 7

THE HEART OF IT ALL

The Christian life was never intended to be a doctrinal movement, nor was the church meant to be a theological institution. The church was birthed to be a kingdom movement that engaged society and brought hope and freedom. It was to inspire a complete spiritual transformation so that the tangibility of God would become an everyday reality. It was to make it possible for us to have a relationship with God and enjoy unrestricted access to Him.

The kingdom is to make faith so real that the aftereffects transform cultures and bring the reality of heaven to earth. It was never about certain prayers or songs, the clothes we wear, or the version of the Bible we read from. The heart of Christianity was and always is—*Jesus*. When He becomes the focus, everything comes into proper alignment. It becomes not about *doing* but *being*—letting His life become the fruit of our life.

We can to often complicate things and make them issues when really they're not. We can use our voice to stir up trouble and cause division that leads to arguments—all in the name of standing for "truth"—when our words are supposed to bring life, peace, and hope.

I have seen the church engage in doctrinal wars, argue truth, and try hard to control what's happening outside its cocoons/spiritual bubbles, looking with critical eyes at how "sinful" everything is (of which I was a part). I can't remember once discussing how we could serve our community, remove the walls we easily put up, or simply be challenged with compassion and how to love people well. Let's not forget personal holiness, which for the most part was all about self-works!

The moment we take something from its intended purpose, we create imbalance and confusion. It's never about the noise we make or the stand we take, but the lives we have the privilege to impact. Jesus made His life and heart about people—not projects or opportunities to convert or show off to the world His particular bent of scriptural truth. He purposed for them to encounter and experience His unlimited, abundant life. When we make it about Him (Jesus), everything changes.

POWER THOUGHT:

We say a lot about ourselves by the things we leave behind.

PERSONAL REFLECTION: What kind of mark does your faith leave?

Day 8

IS IT ALWAYS
ABOUT BEING RIGHT?

M ost people I talk to, including myself, don't really like to be told what to do. Suggestions and advice are one thing, but when you're presented with *this is it*, with little or no options, things can get tense. Growing up in a church culture, I often found myself in that very predicament. I don't know if it was a personality issue, not fitting into a box, or failing to live up to certain expectations. I want to say with all certainty that God is never like that. He is never threatened by our questions; in fact, He welcomes them. He doesn't insist on things being done a certain way.

God isn't angry or grumpy. He is willing for us to figure things out, go through the process, make adjustments along the way, and learn through our mistakes and experiences. I think the church ought to have handful of chill pills! We tend to get bent out of shape when our faith is challenged or when we're faced with different opinions or even trains of thought —often resulting in stiff mindedness and judgmentalism.

It's not always about being right. Listen carefully—if it was, Jesus would have consumed His time on earth by debating and confronting everything that challenged Him. Jesus never presented Himself as one who had "arrived." Nope! He insisted on building relationships and manifesting heaven's reality in everyday life. He wasn't about confronting but connecting, He wasn't about arguing but listening and lending a hand. He wasn't about defending His position but helping others with theirs. His greatest passion was for people to know, live, and experience His dynamic, abundant, and totally fulfilling life.

Jesus never ignored people who thought or believed differently than Him, but He continually invested in them— even if it caused a mark on His own reputation. He was driven by passion and motivated to give life, hope, and freedom to those around Him. He believed in their best and cheered them on in spite of their issues. He offered His grace and power to push through the struggles in life. Here's a thought to ponder: Have we been sending the wrong message? Could it be that the church has spent too much of its time letting the people around them know what they're against, what they want changed, or what they think is wrong? Have we done this instead of connecting, caring, serving, and building relationships with the people around us with the same kind of passion as Jesus had? I don't want us to send the wrong message, create the wrong perception of God, or misrepresent His mission!

It has never been about us (never). It has never been about our particular system, doctrinal beliefs, or our understanding of right and wrong. It has *always been about Him*. And when people encounter *Him*, everything changes.

POWER THOUGHT:

Sometimes it's better to be silent than to open our mouth and send the wrong message.

PERSONAL REFLECTION: What are some ways that can keep you from sending the wrong message?

Day 9

ODDS WITH THE SYSTEM

The thing that amazes me about Jesus is that He was never about a religious system. So many times He would leave the religious community speechless or in frenzy because He simply worked outside the lines. I think it's natural to create systems, because for the most part (let's be honest), we like to control things. The best way to control things is to have a set of rules that people are required to follow—and let's not forget to mention 'the consequences'! You then have a platform on which to determine who is expendable and who is not, who is right or wrong on particular issues or practices. Unfortunately, the church is often thought to work on the same principles, because that's what systems create.

I agree that there needs to be structure or boundaries—not based on performance or duty but on respect, honour, and genuine relationship. Much of the system (if we're honest) is based on our comfort levels, our particular set of beliefs, or our own understanding of the Bible. I think we do real injustice when we allow our frame of reference or theological position to be based on our personal outlook. This can be tragic. No one group has the in scoop— we are all in process. The heart and ministry of Jesus was never segregation or exclusion.

That's what made Jesus different! He welcomed dialogue, and He wasn't bent out of shape with the everyday people He encountered who had different belief systems or values. He purposefully and powerfully valued and loved them. That's the mandate and mission we have the privilege to live out with the people and community around us. I believe the church is intended to be everything Jesus was and is, and once we get hold of that, it will change everything. Success is measured in relationships we build, people we serve, and impacts we leave.

Many of us can quote scripture like it was going out of style, hold to some persuasive beliefs, or place our spirituality in a neat package that says we've got it together, but when it comes to what really matters—the people around us in our communities...we miss it!! That's where our heart, actions, and attitudes speak the loudest.

Jesus dripped heaven and impacted those He encountered, and more often than not, it left Him at odds with the system.

POWER THOUGHT:

Success is measured by the relationships we build, people we serve, and impacts we leave.

PERSONAL REFLECTION: How does your faith put you at odds with the system?

Day 10

GUILT OR CONVICTION?

think we can confuse the words "guilt" and "conviction" without really working hard at it; in fact, in many cases we may not see a real difference. Growing up in church culture, I was led to believe that unless you felt guilt, change would only be temporary. Guilt was everywhere! It was in the preaching, Bible classes, youth group, and everyday get-togethers with other Christians.

I think guilt was intended to motivate us to do right, yet, ironically, it condemns us at the same time. It was used as a way of controlling and keeping people in line. Let's face it —guilt and its close cousin, shame, can be powerful motivators. I have found that guilt works effectively for a time, but eventually people get weary and discouraged of trying so hard to do the right thing. We must realize that pleasing the people around us is a daunting task. It's exhausting and completely useless in the end.

I have learned while walking with God, that guilt and conviction, are two very different things. When we discover that Jesus frees us from guilt and shame, we re-learn or junk a lot of our theology. Guilt brings change (absolutely), but it's the wrong kind of change and for the wrong reasons. So many lives have been devastated and left a trail of debris because of it. That's not the heart Jesus. He always liberated and spoke to the community and the people around Him in a way that brought freedom from guilt or shame.

Guilt at its core speaks to actions or deeds, while conviction speaks to the heart. Jesus is all about the heart! When a person is convicted, something shifts on the inside. It's not about being aware of what we're doing wrong or where we are failing, but rather it's about revealing God's best to us—who He says we are and all the potential He sees in us. This results in a change of heart, because we now begin to see ourselves like He does! Jesus has always been about the heart and *never* about pressure, guilt, or shame.

His words are *always* life and freedom, so everything we believe, say, or do ought to have the same flavour as Him. Anytime our belief system instills fear, guilt, shame, condemnation, panic, inadequacies, or anything other than hope, life, or freedom, it needs to be junked and tossed as garbage. So get rid of guilt and let your convictions be the same as His.

POWER THOUGHT:
The right conviction always leads to the right direction.

PERSONAL REFLECTION: In what way have fear, guilt, and shame affected you?

Day 11

SO YOU FAILED

think we have to learn to look at our failures differently (I'm serious). I'm not talking about the ones we knowingly and willing step into. I'm talking about when we wipe out, when the pressures get the better of us, or when we lose our footing from handling too much. I think most of us have been victims of "good meaning" people who seize moments like that and pounce, desperately wanting/offering to provide us with all the right answers as to why things are going wrong and how to make them right. They may even throw a scripture or two into the mix, which usually (let's face it) just makes things worse.

First, God isn't like that, and secondly, tell those people to go fly a kite. Really, they are just trying to take attention away from their own shortcomings or mess. There will always be people with a Bible larger than life—looking, correcting, and finding ways to 'help' us and others along the way. (Thanks but *no* thanks.) All of us are on a journey, and failing is a part of the process.

Listen, **failing never disqualifies us**! In fact, it sets us up for breakthrough and success. We've got to learn to turn this thing around and take full advantage of the times we fail. We can't let the voices of criticism, even our own cynicism, get the best of us. God is *always* for us! Think of it this way—without those failures, we wouldn't enjoy the benefits of success. When you think about it, how can you really trust someone who has never walked through life experiences? Struggles and obstacles are never there to break us but to propel us into the next realm of victory and personal experiences.

We tend to want the finished product or the end result right now, but we forget that the end result or the finish product *always* involves a process. When we begin to see the process as just as important as the end result, we'll begin to unleash our God-given potential. We were born to soar, but before we can soar, we have to leave the nest, step out, and take risks. We must try, learn, and—you guessed it—fail. Listen, that doesn't mean that we're failures (not at all) ... we're just learning and in process.

There's no room for "know it alls," people who think they've "arrived," or any other form of spiritual elitism— there's enough hot air already going around to have to deal with that. The true formula for success is always being willing to learn through our mistakes and make the necessary adjustments along the way. There is then *no* room for finger pointing, comparisons, or thinking we are better than the next—*nope!* Rather, we can help each other along the way.

POWER THOUGHT:

Never be intimated by failure; use it as springboard to propel you forward.

PERSONAL REFLECTION: What are some ways you can benefit from the times you fail?

Day 12

"WOULD DO"
AND ACTUALLY "DID"

The Bible is full of stories and experiences that involved people from all walks of life: Kings, Queens, ranchers, fishermen, tax collectors, business owners, and everyone in between. As far as Jesus was concerned, everyone mattered, everyone had a purpose, and everyone was valued. In fact, He went out of His way to connect with them. We can learn so much about people simply by watching their actions, body language, and how they speak/interact with others. If a person takes a close look at Jesus – wow – we can learn enough to carry us through a lifetime!

Some years ago, the slogan WWJD (What Would Jesus Do?) flooded the Christian community. A person could buy bracelets, necklaces, bookmarks, and all kinds of other merchandise graced by these letters. I know that the intention was honourable, but it was confusing at the same time. If you have been exposed to church or any kind of Christian culture, you've definitely noticed that there are a lot of different opinions, practices, and even beliefs. The question shouldn't be about what Jesus *would have done* but what Jesus *did*. You see, what Jesus did changes everything—it stops confusion, misunderstanding, personal opinions, and even religious bias.

What Jesus did was to reach into the lives of people, no matter their background or belief system. What He did was to unlock people's potential, offering them a whole new perspective and a brand new, transformed life. He instilled hope and made no distinction based on colour, race, or culture. What He did was bring freedom! Freedom from condemnation and the demands of the religious. It was a completely open invitation to a personal relationship with Him that had nothing to do with *religion* or church affiliation of any kind.

Most of us are familiar with the expression, "actions speak louder than words." Jesus's actions showed the world that He was the real deal. His actions settled all confusion and arguments. If we make what Jesus did our focus, misunderstandings will be clarified.

Doing what Jesus did will take you out of your comfort zone, stretch you, expand your thinking, and bring you to places you've never been before. In fact, doing what Jesus did will change everything about you. It will change your purpose, your passion, and your interactions with others. Even your mission will never be the same!

POWER THOUGHT:
Actions will speak louder than words.

PERSONAL REFLECTION: How has what Jesus did influence you to do what you do?

Day 13

FORGIVING YOURSELF

I'm sure all of us have been in a place at one time or another where we've had the opportunity to forgive someone. Let's be honest here and say that forgiveness is not an easy subject. It usually involves hurt, disappointment, or even emotional damage. This is understandable, because the things people say or do (including ourselves) can really take a toll on a person's life. So when we talk about forgiveness, it can raise eyebrows and even cause pushback from people. Forgiveness can be a tough and touchy subject.

Let's shift that for a moment. What about forgiving ourselves? This is one topic that we really don't consider or give the attention it deserves, but dealing with this will help us deal with the other —even though it can be the *hardest*. Once we learn to forgive ourselves, we actually become better at forgiving others.

Too often we can be quick to beat ourselves up and hold ourselves to a standard we can never meet, and then we wonder why we move from disappointment to frustration in so many situations. Learning to value, respect, and forgive ourselves is part of living to our fullest potential as God designed us to do. Do we make mistakes? Do we wipe out? Do we do things that we wish we hadn't? Absolutely! But that should never define who we are. Forgiveness is a freeing experience—not to avoid responsibility but to take responsibility, giving ourselves the grace to learn from it and then to move forward.

Listen, we can't afford to stay stuck, because life is way too short and relationships are far too valuable. We have got to learn to be in the habit of forgiving ourselves and others around us. Bitterness and self-condemnation only make matters worse. Our lives are too important to miss God's best.

Life can definitely throw us for a loop, people can get really hurt, and we can do a lot of harm when we don't respect ourselves. So we have got to learn to love, serve, and forgive. It won't just impact the people around us—it will transform us in the process!

POWER THOUGHT:

Forgiveness isn't always easy, but it liberates your potential.

PERSONAL REFLECTION: What are some ways unforgiveness is holding you back?

Day 14

U-TURNS

Who likes U-turns? They're usually frustrating and annoying, for the simple fact that they can remind us we're headed in the wrong direction or that we missed a turn we needed to take. In the world of GPS technology, a person should never get lost or miss a turn (so you would think)! We've become so accustomed to technology, we can easily forget to think about what we're doing.

Technology is truly wonderful, as long as it works properly. We are so dependent on our little devices, so when the power fails, the batteries die, or the WIFI connection is lost, we get lost. We live in a world where we can have five hundred friends that we contact regularly without actually being with them. We can turn lights on, change the temperature in the room, or view what's happening on the other side of the world with just a couple of clicks. So why is it that we still find ourselves missing a turn or heading in the wrong direction?

The reality of God's presence is often lost in the shuffle of life. When dealing with pressure and expectations, a person can easily feel lost and overwhelmed. Missing a turn or heading in the wrong direction can naturally be the result. It's no wonder we can find ourselves confused, lost, or even wondering where we are and what the heck is going on. U-turns are often unavoidable. You and I were never meant to work under stress and unbearable pressure, yet we may find our ourselves at that place more often than not.

God has designed us to succeed, to push through, and to overcome our challenges. It's the challenges (not the stress) in our lives that pave the way for possibility and contribute to our growth and success! During WWII, Sir Winston Churchill went to bed every night looking at a map of Britain to see where they were the most vulnerable to enemy attacks. He didn't look at the map to see weakness but to find the opportunities, see the possibilities, and believed they would overcome. Many times, he called the nation to pray because he knew that involving God would bring a perspective and realization that they were bigger than the odds and would overcome. It's important to know that with God, the road is full of endless possibilities and overcome-able odds.

It's easy to give up, get overwhelmed, and lose heart, but we've got to remind ourselves that God is so much bigger than any of the mistakes we make. He is much bigger than the odds we think are stacked against us. And He is so much bigger than our "missed turns" or misdirection. So never be afraid of U-turns —make them! Make them often. It's never about having it all together or being perfect. It's about the process and making adjustments along the way. That's how we learn! That's how we grow! That's how we become the people that God has designed us to be.

POWER THOUGHT:

U-Turns never steal momentum; rather, they set you up for greater opportunities.

PERSONAL REFLECTION: How have you let setbacks influence your direction?

Day 15

LETTING BYGONES
BE BYGONES

think most people find it natural to hang on to "stuff!" We seem to hang on to our mistakes and our hurts. We hang on to things that haven't worked out in our favour, or whatever negative experiences we've come up against. All of us have been disappointed or frustrated at one time or another. What we do with that disappointment or frustration is very important. The easiest way of dealing with it is simply to bury it, only to have it come back and bite us down the road.

Emotions are powerful, and when they're directed in the right way, they can transform and influence not only ourselves but the people around us in incredible ways. Learning to "let go" can be one of the most difficult things for any person to do. After all, isn't letting go the same as admitting defeat? Not at all! That's a lie we often buy into. We think that by letting go, we show that we don't care, that it doesn't really matter, we're giving up or, worse yet, we're wrong! But in fact, "letting go" can be one of the most effective ways to free and propel us into what's ahead.

Life will always have bumps, struggles, and roadblocks. But when we learn to let go (let bygones be bygones), we free ourselves from the misery and bondage of the hurts and frustrations that hold us back. Many times, we just don't realize that by hanging on to these things, we harm ourselves in the end. We can't change the people or the situations around us, but we can change ourselves and the things that we hold on to.

Being free is a powerful reality and one that we are designed by God to live in and experience. But to step into this reality, we need to "let go" of all the negative things we tend to hang on to.

Paul, one of the preeminent writers of the New Testament, found the secret to this dilemma. He wrote, "but I focus on one thing :forgetting the past and looking forward to what lies ahead, I press on..." (Philippians 3:13b,14a NLT). I love that, because sometimes we need to be more aggressive at "letting things go" in our lives and freeing ourselves to move into the future. Paul was coming from the perspective that his life still needed work. (He hadn't arrived, he was in process.) But his secret to moving ahead with his life in the midst of that process was to let go.

Letting go isn't always about forgetting. That is the misconception! There are things we may never forget, nor should we. It's about not allowing those things to hinder us in our journey or hold us back from the good things ahead.

The future is ours to discover, and the present is for us to utilize and manage, so let's learn from our experiences, our mistakes, and even our failures. Let's refuse to let those negative things paralyze us and stop us from moving forward! Let's learn to let "bygones be bygones!"

POWER THOUGHT:
Letting go is part of the process of moving you forward.

PERSONAL REFLECTION: What is it that you're allowing to hold you back?

Day 16

INADEQUACIES

This is a big one! No, I mean, this is a REALLY *big* one! Nothing stops us dead in our tracks faster than the feeling that we don't measure up or, even worse, that we don't have what it takes! Far too often we rob ourselves of the truth that we can accomplish great things, because we have listened to all the wrong voices telling us that we can't. (And let's be honest here, sometimes the voices are our own.)

Feeling inadequate paralyzes us, holds us back, restricts us, and keeps us from exploring, dreaming, and believing that all things are possible. We were created by God to soar, dream, and reach our destiny! Tragically, we stay stuck where we are and settle for less because we believe what we've been told. Our story is too familiar. We've been told that we can't, it won't work, or we need to stop thinking that way! So instead of being empowered to soar, we get deflated, and we are immobilized.

Jesus's whole mission and purpose was to empower us to be who we were created to be. There will always be naysayers, people who see only our mistakes. The world (and even the church) usually has more than enough of those kinds of people to go around. So let's not get sidetracked or fall into the trap of comparing ourselves to anyone around us.

You and I are unique. There is no one else like us in the whole world, and when we feel inadequate, we are trying to fit into another person's mould or expectations. But how can we? We're different, and we bring a different set of tools and experiences to the table. It's time to celebrate who we are and put our inadequacies behind us. So what if we can't do what others can? We can also do what others can't.

It's easy to lose hope when we focus on what others say or when we try to live up to other's expectations. We need to forget that nonsense, otherwise we'll never achieve our destiny, no matter how hard we try. We have to learn to be who we are and to stop making excuses as to why we aren't who we should be. You and I will never feel inadequate if we stick to who God created us to be. Jesus is our model and our greatest example. So let's soar, chase our dreams, and be everything we were created to be.

POWER THOUGHT:
Those who speak the loudest don't always need to be heard.

PERSONAL REFLECTION: How have you let the voices around you stop you from moving ahead?

Day 17

ARE WE AS ADVERTISED?

We all have baggage of some kind or another—stuff we keep hidden from people around us as we try to make ourselves look better than we actually are. *Image is king* in our society. We see it everywhere we look. It's easy to get swallowed up by it or get tangled up in it one way or another if we're not careful. So much of life carries expectations, and you're easily ignored or shoved to the side if you're not fitting in with what's going on around you.

These pressures that have invaded our culture, society, and even our faith communities have created a mountain of casualties. Why? Because we can never keep up. That kind of life will continue to spin us in circles until we fly off the merry-go-round. Jesus addressed this very thing when he said that we become a slave to whatever masters us. In other words, we are controlled by the things that influence us most.

Perception is powerful. How we want people to see us can often be misleading and create a real bondage. Church culture is notorious for that (breaks my heart). We have spiritual answers for every situation, and maintaining that image has devastating results. It's like we've created a society in which we have to live a lie, but we can only maintain that for so long before the crash, leaving us to wonder what in the world went wrong.

The good news is we **never** have to stay in that upside-down pattern! We don't have to submit to those pressures, nor do we have to become casualties to this sort of life. We don't have to pretend any longer. It's normal to want to do well and not disappoint; in fact, those are God-given desires. But we get off track when we hide from being real and work hard to make our life look *imaged up*.

Letting go of false perceptions, losing the polished appearance, and taking ownership of our feelings are key to our freedom. We've got to learn to be happy with ourselves (mistakes and all) and celebrate our journey. No one person has it all put together, no matter how polished it may look. Celebrate your life, your journey, and the process you're in.

POWER THOUGHT:

Being real and authentic is the blueprint to freedom.

PERSONAL REFLECTION: What are some ways you find yourself hiding behind false pretenses?

Day 18

SHORT-CUTS

I remember when the Rubik's cube first hit the market and really took off. Everyone had to have one! It was amazing to watch people take a jumbled-up mess of mixed-up colours and, after spinning and twisting it in all directions, eventually match the different colours to all six sides of the cube. There was definitely an art to it, and many people mastered it, but I found it much easier to just take the coloured stickers off and re-arrange it that way.

Why is it that we often look for the easy way of doing things? Why do we take short-cuts to get things done? The Rubik's cube could be conquered, but it took time and you had to learn to move things around in the right sequence (which I could never figure out, by the way).

I think we live in a time-driven era (get in, get it done, and get out). We tend not to stick around and push through some of the real hard things. I'll be the first to admit that I don't like getting stuck or having my brain freeze up when I feel lost in situations. Taking the stickers off and re-arranging them seems to be the more logical thing to do. But by taking that short-cut, we rob ourselves of conquering and overcoming the obstacle, and we short-change the process!

Obstacles are *never* the problem! In fact, obstacles are an opportunity! We short-change ourselves by not learning to push through them. There's no doubt that short-cuts are easier, but at the end of the day, they rob us of the opportunity to grow and overcome. Just like our muscles are built by pushing thru resistance, our character is one of the most precious aspects of who we are, and it's built by pushing through and overcoming the obstacles in front of us! We were created by God to push through. Every one of us has that ability to find the sequence and learn to do things the right way… that's how we Grow!

There's a verse in the Bible that speaks to this very principle. In fact, it's a theme you can find all through scripture. This particular verse was written by a follower of Jesus who walked thru his share of trouble and truly understood this principle. He tells us to be excited about *every* obstacle that comes, because they will change our character and elevate us to the next level. (James ch.1:2-4)

Remember, it's never about the short-term gain but about getting it to sink so deep that it changes the very fabric of our life. Like the Rubik's cube, nothing happens until we see what might look like a disorganized mess and then learning the sequence to conquer and overcome by pushing through! Let's not ignore the opportunities around us. Let's face the fact that we don't usually have to look very far, because they somehow seem to find us. (Just hang around certain people for three or four minutes and you'll have your opportunity.) I'm learning that attitudes can always be adjusted, and perspectives can always be flipped. We can choose different words to come out of our mouths, and our reactions can always be re-adjusted!

POWER THOUGHT:

Don't short change the process, Growth comes by pushing through.

PERSONAL REFLECTION: What are some ways in which you've taken a short-cut, thinking it would get you to the end faster?

Day 19

WHEN IT DOESN'T SEEM TO WORK

How many times have we tried something and no matter what we do, it just doesn't work? Frustration builds! Our blood begins to boil, or we just throw up our hands and walk away. Yet in the back of our minds, we know it's not over. We know it's possible! So what do we do?

In moments like these, I don't always know the solution. Sometimes we find that there are more questions than answers. It's frustrating, disappointing, irritating, and, at times, deflating. We've all been there at one time or another and felt powerless. We take it personally, and we feel that we don't have what it takes. We think we've failed or that the world is against us. Unfortunately, that always leads us to a dead end.

Too often, we guilt ourselves or use some past excuse we've picked up along the way. Life will hand us those kinds of moments at times. No one volunteers for them or looks forward to having them show up. That's why we need the *right* kind of people in our lives—the kind of people who lend a hand rather than point a finger. These are the people who provide a clearer perspective, who give us life and don't contribute to the frustrating situations in front of us. These are the people who encourage us, who don't suck out the little bit of energy we have left.

People usually mean well, but we may wonder about that sometimes. It's the people who come alongside us *in the middle of the situation*, when we're up against the wall, that make the difference. It's not necessarily about trying harder or doing things over and over again. It's about listening and learning through the process. So when it doesn't seem to work, we need to take a step back. We need to invite others into our process, because they have a different set of eyes. Sometimes, their viewpoint reveals the answer we've been looking for.

We've all heard the saying, "Rome wasn't built in a day." And it wasn't. It took a team of people who were committed through the process—ups and downs, banged up fingers, bruises, aches and pains, highs and lows! When things just aren't working, let's learn to not give up, don't get down on ourselves, don't get discouraged or disappointed. Remember, God has provided all the answers. Sometimes we just need to take a step back, invite Him and others into the process, and learn to make the right kind of adjustments!

POWER THOUGHT:

It's not always about what you have but **who** you have around you.

PERSONAL REFLECTION: What are some ways you can benefit from the people God has put around you?

Day 20

COVERING UP

Sometimes we think that the safest thing to do is to cover up! We fear exposure, people's reactions, or admitting we have a problem. But this is counter-productive and will only serve to harm us in the long run. Most of us have examples of that in our past, which just solidifies our desire to cover things up! We don't realize that things just pile up and do even greater damage in the long run. Many of us have been burned often enough from our past experience that we simply avoid these situations.

The misconception, however, is that by hiding or covering up, these things will disappear or sort themselves out down the road. But truth be told they only get bigger and come back to haunt us later on. God's intention is for every one of us to be free. As far as God is concerned, freedom is not a luxury (for only a few) but a by-product of **His** grace in our everyday life. His grace isn't worked for or earned by some religious nonsense that never really deals with the issues. It's a grace that uncovers the hurts, messes, and failures. He restores and rebuilds who we were meant to be in the first place!

God is *never* about exposure! He *never* sees our weaknesses or failures the way we do. He sees beyond them! He is *never* disappointed or runs out of patience. He is thrilled to walk alongside us, leading us to victory and freedom! In fact, everything about Him is for our benefit and complete well-being!

So the path to freedom is *never* about covering up but about opening up. It's about being honest with ourselves and facing the things we normally want to hide (things we hope will simply take care of themselves). Jesus has the answers, and when we open up, He promises to visit those areas that we're afraid of. He's right there to heal those hurts and wounded places, breathing His life into each and every one of them! Healing our hearts is what He is a master at!

This isn't just about opening up and giving these things to Jesus but letting Him have control of them in the first place, before all the damage is done. He already knows everything about us, and He's still willing to go out of His way to help. He *never* fails! He *never* disappoints! He *never* over-promises and under-delivers. He is a miracle worker, and there is *nothing* He can't do! It's *never* just about meeting Him halfway. When we're serious, open, and real, He comes all the way to meet us where we are!

POWER THOUGHT:

How you view what you're going through affects your progress in getting there.

PERSONAL REFLECTION: What are the things hindering you from your destination?

Day 21

BACKTRACKING

don't know of anybody who likes to backtrack. We start out in a certain direction, and lo and behold, we find out somewhere down the road (and that can sometimes be hours down the road) that we missed a turn … *oops!* Now we're going to have to backtrack. Not much fun; in fact, it can be deflating and disheartening, all at the same time. In moments like these, we usually find ourselves asking, "Why didn't I pay more attention?" or "How could I have missed it?" That's okay, because we all have moments like that, no matter how much planning we do.

Circumstances and life situations often come to us unannounced. In fact, they can completely catch us off guard. In moments like that, we often find ourselves scrambling or backtracking simply to get our bearings. We end up spinning in circles, wondering "What am I going to do now?" More often than not, we find ourselves making decisions in the midst of that whirlwind of frustration and disappointment, ultimately making the situation even worse.

God never meant for us to live in the spiral of those events but to press on through them. David, one of Israel's most famous and influential kings, summed it up pretty well when he said, "even though I walk through the darkest valley" (backtracking can be one of those times), "I will not be afraid." And why? "For you (God) are with me." Did you notice that he said, "walk through"? We don't live there but simply pass through! That means moments, not a lifetime.

Backtracking is part of life. At times, we'll find ourselves doing that very thing. I don't think it's about avoiding those moments but learning to navigate through them when they come. Our attitude has a powerful role to play, and if we simply adjust it, our outcome will be completely changed! God designed us to overcome whatever comes against us. Backtracking isn't the big deal that we often think it is—it's just a part of the process!

Life is full of opportunities, and backtracking presents us with one of them. As long as we see our life this way, we will *never* become casualties; instead, it will bring the best out of us! Let's learn to embrace those opportunities so we can help turn them into our victories, not our defeats. **God is with us**, and that's the game changer. We really have **nothing** to fear. Let's make the most of those backtracking moments, because there's more power in our testimony than we realize!

POWER THOUGHT:

There is always more to the story then what we often are willing to see.

PERSONAL REFLECTION: What are some ways we can
stay the course when we find ourselves sidetracked by everything around us?

Day 22

WORRY

We all know, at least in principle, that worry never benefits us. In fact, statistics prove that usually the stuff we worry about never actually happens. Worry does two very negative things: it robs us of our focus and it takes away hope. We need to understand that focus and hope are extremely important to our success in life. Our lives are greatly influenced or impacted by what we focus on the most, and hope is the foundation that gets us through, even when life looks impossible. Focus and hope are the keys to how we live, experience events, and see our future.

Far too often we're inundated by the negative, by the *what if's* or what we think is going to happen—so much so that we lose the ability to decipher between the facts and our emotions. Life is full of unpredictable situations, and too often worry becomes the norm. Jesus taught that we are not to worry. So much in life grabs our attention. Our thoughts, attitudes, and beliefs are so powerful that our everyday experiences are affected by them.

God intends for us to live and experience life to the full, and that will always involve focus and hope. Distractions are unavoidable, that's for certain. We don't even necessarily have to look for them, because they find us! So focusing on the right things is absolutely crucial. We face choices every day, and the ability to choose what occupies our thoughts is on us! God promises to help us in our weaknesses, so trusting Him to guide us in this process is a game changer. And that, in turn, births **hope**!!

Hope is our fuel. When hope is alive, we are not easily moved. Hope is powerful; it breathes life into us! Hope keeps us stable when everything around us is moving and shaking. It overrides the clouded areas and provides a perspective that keeps us above the things that try to pull us underneath. Right focus births hope, so what we build our hope on is very important. When we find our mind distracted, discouraged, or disappointed, we've got to keep our attention on the right things. Jesus provides everything we need, and developing a relationship with Him is a powerful way to build our hope and bring proper focus to life.

The scriptures are full of wisdom, insight, and powerful perspectives, not only for providing the right focus, but for helping us see through the distractions, frustrations, hurts, and disappointments that come our way. They provide the right foundation and give us true hope that will have us soaring above whatever comes our way.

POWER THOUGHT:

Worry doesn't change a thing; it simply focuses your attention on things that don't really matter.

PERSONAL REFLECTION: What are the things, events, or experiences in your life that cause you to worry?

Day 23

FACE TO FACE
WITH TROUBLE

I'm sure most of us have experienced car trouble at some point in our life. On our recent trip to Arizona, we experienced "troubles," and let me emphasize the plural! Not only did we get a flat tire on the way, but the "check engine" light came on. This usually isn't such a bad issue, but this one was —every time our car went up any kind of incline, it would start jerking like it wasn't getting the fuel it needed to keep up with the speed. The farther we travelled, the worse it got. So after back and forth phone calls, we got hold of a service garage that would look at the problem. We found out that four out of the six cylinders were misfiring. That's a problem! The car was getting the right amount of fuel, but it wasn't firing correctly. So, $360 USD later, we were back on the road, problem solved.

In the middle of that problem (and there were many more that took place), the feelings of frustration and helplessness were overwhelming. Most of us like it when things work the way they're supposed to, so when they don't, it can affect our performance and create havoc with our emotions. Life is often like that. Things don't always work out perfectly. Issues surface and at times we'll be confronted with "performance" issues. What we do in times like that is very significant.

Upsets, setbacks, difficulties, and unfavourable situations are a part of life, and how we handle them, by making the right adjustments, changes how we travel through life. I've recognized that there is no one pill that fixes every situation. At times in our journey, our "check engine" light will come on. We can't necessarily prevent the things that happen; however, we can change what we do in the middle of them.

We are uniquely created by God and have the power to make decisions and necessary adjustments as we experience life situations. Our attitudes can always be adjusted. We are never abandoned, left to figure things out on our own (although it may feel like it at times), or punished for something we did or didn't do. We have the Holy Spirit to draw on in times like that. The Bible teaches that He helps us in our weakness (or times of helplessness).

Never be threatened by issues that come up. Don't be hard on yourself if you struggle when situations arise. Let's allow ourselves to process and work things through, adapting and making the necessary adjustments along the way, because it's moments like that where we see God's provision and our character develops and changes in the middle of our troubles.

POWER THOUGHT:

Always allow yourself the space to make necessary adjustments along the way.

PERSONAL REFLECTION: How have you learned to navigate through the difficult situations in life?

Day 24

FINDING PURPOSE

Many of us struggle with finding purpose. We don't necessarily hate life, but at times we can struggle with enjoying it. Purpose is one of those things we don't get taught in a classroom; rather, it's birthed out of our experiences in life. It's an over-flow of our passions and our desire to make a difference in the lives of people. We want to leave our mark, or simply contribute to what's going on around us in a meaningful way.

Purpose is powerful! It gets us up in the morning, and it fuels why we do what we do! It provides goals to aim for and the energy to accomplish them. So when those things aren't there, life often becomes more about routine and duty. As a result, we have no drive to push into what's coming next. We can all dream, have interests, or set goals. We can even be passionate about things and desire to contribute to those things in life. But when circumstances don't work out, or we hit a series of roadblocks or are confronted with unforeseen events, it can really throw a wrench into things.

Life will have those moments, and when we aren't ready or prepared, it can really rock our world. It's in times like these where life becomes challenging and, if left unchecked, can spiral in a negative direction. That's why purpose is so important. In times like these, purpose provides what's needed to carry us through. The Bible is full of examples of people filled with passions, goals, and the ability to leave their mark. They made a difference in their world, and it was purpose that fueled their pursuits and helped chart their pathways through life, even when unforeseen circumstances took them by surprise.

Too often, we try to find purpose, but it can't be found through self-effort, strenuous work, or striving to get hold of it. It's simply an **overflow** of our experiences. Passions grow as we experience what we love, enjoy, or find fulfilling. Those things are all God-given, and He above all wants us to experience life to the fullest. Having purpose is the key to fulfillment, too many of us are living life unfulfilled. Living life this way brings disappointment after disappointment and let-down after let-down. It's that routine that causes a lack of purpose to prevail.

We need to learn to grab hold of the things God has given us. We need to challenge our current perspectives and make ourselves aware of the things that are going our way. It all starts with that shift, and then it begins to grow as we become more aware. Our heavenly Father is our biggest fan, and reaching out to Him in our purposelessness moments can provide the hope we need to bring about those changes. You and I are far too important to let life just pass us by. We really need to grab hold of life and make it matter!

POWER THOUGHT:

Purpose is never a struggle; rather, it's an overflow of what I value most.

PERSONAL REFLECTION: How does having purpose in your life affect how you do things?

Day 25

CONQUERING GIANTS

Giants are those things or situations in life that hinder or hold us back. They can be fears, insecurities, unhealthy mind-sets that we've developed, and beliefs about ourselves or others. They can be as small as seemingly insignificant offences or as large as unforgiveness that we carry around like excess baggage. Nobody likes being in bondage, yet so much of life can be seriously affected by these realities if we allow them into our lives.

God's design for us is not only to experience complete freedom but to live it as a natural experience, just like breathing. Yet so often it can seem to be a distant reality in our lives. Giants, ironically, are a normal part of life. Facing them is natural, but how we deal with them determines how we overcome them. Every one of us can conquer them if we learn to recognize them when they surface. You and I are equipped to deal with our giants, so understanding why they're there is important to our growth and progress in life.

Understanding that giants aren't necessarily negative is an important fact. In fact, they provide the platform we need to push through and elevate to new heights in life. Are they fun? Absolutely not! Are they frustrating? They sure can be! Are they persistent? They most certainly are! But when we break their hold on us and push through what seems like too big of an obstacle, we overcome their grip on us, and it changes everything.

We were created by God to overcome, to conquer, and to defeat every last one of them. Does it happen overnight? Nope, it sure doesn't. It's a process of learning and identifying these giants and going after them, armed with the truth. We need to learn through each of our experiences so that we can apply it to the next time another one of those giants appears. Then we can help others reach that same point.

Giants come in all shapes and sizes, but their purpose and their end goal are always the same. Understanding that *we can conquer* them is critical, because they will yell and scream and intimidate, taking up our full attention so that we feel trapped and doubtful that we can ever beat them. God has given us everything we need, and more, to experience the fullness of life. Conquering our giants is a necessary part of experiencing that fullness, so how we look at those giants is vital. Fear, insecurity, self-doubt, inadequacy, and shame are all giants that can be conquered. Remember, God has given us all we need to conquer all of those things!

POWER THOUGHT:

Obstacles are not necessarily problems in our way but opportunities for us to overcome.

PERSONAL REFLECTION: How have you allowed

giants to stand in your way instead of using them as a platform to get you through what's ahead of you?

Day 26

THE JESUS I NEVER KNEW

The Jesus I grew up with in my "religious culture" was often portrayed as a villain. I'm sure that wasn't the intent, but it was often the reality. I learned early on that He was quick to punish. Your performance, or lack of it, would constitute the degree to which you would feel His wrath. We were often scared into things to avoid His anger. Then there was the pressure to be careful, to be very aware, because the enemy was going to deceive and trap us in some evil false teaching, deception, or sin.

Needless to say, it painted a very distorted picture of who Jesus really is. I'm thankful for my experiences (although I still wonder about some), but I have learned over the years that what I was taught and experienced about Jesus wasn't true (thank God). I always felt that I could never measure up, I was always a disappointment, and I could never do enough. Let me say this: "religion" will always confuse! It will always leave you feeling inadequate, and you will always be striving to do more to feel accepted.

In my journey, I have learned and experienced the very opposite, and it has shaped me to be who I am today. Listen, who really wants to hang out with a person who is easily angered? Or who wants to hang out with someone who is constantly looking over their shoulder to see if He approves of what they're doing? How much fun would it be to hang around someone who's quick to chastise or point the finger at us when we do something wrong? Or how about telling us that it's our fault that we're in the middle of the mess we're in? Who wants to be with someone who only helps if we're "committed enough," or "believe right"? To top that all off, some people threaten us with the fires of hell when we don't measure up. Let me say this: hell no, and no thank you!

Much like a recovering alcoholic, a wrong view of Jesus can often be a real process to overcome. It can be a hard and seemingly endless struggle. But I'm telling you, *it is worth it!* Once you discover who Jesus really is, your life and experiences will never be the same! Detoxing from "religious Churchianity" is a powerful, life-changing experience!

Jesus isn't about pointing out wrong or showing us where we are failing. He doesn't make us flounder in guilt, but He does empower us to overcome and experience His transforming, abundant life! He doesn't save us from something but to something. He never reveals our failures, but shows us what He has accomplished on our behalf. He walks with us through the fire—not to expose anything but to show us the way through. He always believes the absolute best of us, and He always brings hope and assurance. He speaks life into **every** situation! That's the **real** Jesus, and that's the Jesus that continues to transform my life.

POWER THOUGHT:

The real Jesus is totally worth pursuing and taking the time to get to know.

PERSONAL REFLECTION: How has what you've been taught created a mess that's extremely hard to overcome?

Day 27

LIFE LESSONS

Back in the day, Kenny Rogers sang a very popular song called, "The Gambler." In that song, there's a line in the chorus that I think conveys some important life principles. Yes, it is country music, and yes, it is old, but hey, you find gold in the most unlikely of places! The chorus talks about knowing when to hold your cards, when to fold them and sometimes it's best just to walk away or to get the heck out of dodge …lol. It goes on to suggest, you should never count your money when you're still at the table but hold on till the game is done.

For many of us, life feels like a gamble. At times, there are many twists and turns that make us wonder. But life is not a gamble! Those twists and turns are opportunities to learn and exercise wisdom! The Bible teaches that wisdom is something we gain through everyday life experiences. For example, the person that counts their money before the game is over isn't wise, because so much can change in a short period of time. Wisdom teaches us when it's time to fold (stop fighting and let things go, walk away, or even run). We can learn so much in life and sometimes its through those times when we don't do the right thing!

The Bible is full of examples of people who failed, made big mistakes, or really blew it, yet they grew in wisdom through the whole process. We've got to learn to chill and relax! It's *never* about perfection or having all our bases covered (that stuff is for fairy tales). Let's face it, there is only one *person* who walked in perfection, and you and I aren't Him, but His DNA is a part of who we are. The potential to learn and to grow to be like Him is a living reality. Because of that, we can always learn through all of life's experiences; in fact, wisdom is a natural by-product of Jesus on the inside of us!

Unlike the title of the Kenny Rogers song, we don't need advice on gambling, but we can go deeper and make our life about exercising wisdom. Wisdom is an open invitation to leave our mark and transform everything about ourselves and the people and situations around us. Wisdom changes how we respond to things. It shapes our future and sets us up for success. Wisdom also affects relationships. It fosters integrity and makes the most of the lessons we learn and apply to life.

Let's not get down on ourselves when we make mistakes or fail at things. Rather, let those experiences serve as life's invaluable lessons so we can utilize (exercising wisdom) what we learn. Life never becomes a drag but always an opportunity full of life-changing experiences.

POWER THOUGHT:

Never stop learning; walking with Jesus is an ongoing, life-changing experience.

PERSONAL REFLECTION: What lessons can you learn through the different twists, turns, and ups and downs of the things in life that come your way?

Day 28

EMBRACING THE STRUGGLE

I don't know too many people who enjoy struggling in life. In fact, most of us go out of our way to avoid it. Yet no matter how hard we try to accomplish this, we never succeed, because whether we like it or not, it's part of life. It's important to understand that God isn't the author of our struggles, nor is He simply using them as a "teaching tool." Struggles come for a variety of reasons: the choices we make, the situations we're in, or simply the events going on in the world around us.

If you're alive and breathing, you will, at some point, experience struggles. What we do in those situations makes all the difference. Embracing our struggles doesn't mean we surrender or give up but that we understand those struggles are there and we're not afraid or threatened by them. Pretending that they're not there, or running away from them, is never the right answer. It's standing tall and facing them that's the key to overcoming them!

Learning something new, admitting that we are wrong, pushing through limitations, facing the unknown, working through circumstances, dealing with people, or looking for answers in a pile of unknowns can be a struggle! But facing them and determining to work through them is how we grow and develop into the people God has designed us to be. Our lives are too valuable, and God's plan and purpose is more than just to survive but to thrive and make the most of life by overcoming these struggles.

We've all heard the phrase, "What doesn't hurt you makes you stronger." Well, that's hogwash! Struggles hurt, and sometimes they leave us floundering; however, when we embrace and work through them we become stronger! The Bible tells us that if God is for us, nothing can stand against us. Struggles are a normal part of life, and they are unavoidable. We may not always understand them, but every one of them is overcome-able!

Embracing our struggles is never a sign of weakness but of strength! It's never an indication of inability but capability. And *never* is it a statement of surrender! It's a declaration that we are grabbing hold of victory! Everything becomes possible because of Jesus!

POWER THOUGHT:

Never be threatened by the struggles of life, because moments like that are designed to build you stronger.

PERSONAL REFLECTION: In what ways do you embrace the struggle and keep yourself from playing the victim?

Day 29

INVISIBLE MEASURING STICK

One of the most destructive patterns we can ever find ourselves in is comparing ourselves to others. I think that if we're honest, many of us have an internal measuring stick that comes out in all sorts of situations and experiences. You never physically see it, but you know it's there. Most of us do it, and too many of us have even become enslaved by it. I think it starts off small, and then grows to a friendly competition, and then, if left unchecked, quickly becomes personal validation!

God has created us all differently. In fact, the Bible uses words like "fearfully and wonderfully made," "knit me together in my mother's womb." We may have similarities, yet we're still very unique. We may have common interests, yet we all have different ways of doing things. Comparing ourselves to others is damaging and leads us into an endless downward spiral. Our lives are far too important to compare ourselves to others.

Too often we measure success by having to be the best or doing things better than others. Companies and corporations (hey, even churches) spend big money to find ways to "outdo the competition." In principle, I understand that, but when it comes to our lives (who we are as individuals), our value and what we contribute should never be compared with others. It always leads to wrong judgements of ourselves and those around us!

We have to learn to celebrate who we are and be grateful for the things God has done. We must learn to be comfortable in our own skin. Does that mean we're going to do everything right, or that we don't need to change or make improvements? Not at all. That's all just part of life! But using the invisible measuring stick and comparing ourselves with others is both unhealthy and destructive! Differences ought never to divide or intimidate us but rather solidify the fact of how important each of us is, and that we need each other.

God doesn't value us because we're like Him or even like those around us. He values us because we're all different and we all bring something different to the grand program. Our uniqueness and our differences are our strengths, and measuring ourselves against others creates an imbalance that leads to disappointment and an unhealthy approach to life. You are you, and I am me! We should never need to compare ourselves to each other. We are God's masterpiece, and there isn't any need for measuring sticks here!

POWER THOUGHT:

You being you, is God's gift to the world.

PERSONAL REFLECTION: In what ways do you find yourself using an invisible measuring stick and comparing yourself to others around you?

Day 30

"INSIDE OUTSIDE, UPSIDE DOWN"

I remember reading a book called *Inside, Outside, Upside Down* when I was fairly young. It's quite an easy read and can probably be finished in under a minute, but it says a lot about life. It's amazing what can be learned from a children's book.

The book takes us through the adventures of a young bear after he climbs into an empty box. The box's lid falls shut, and it gets picked up, turned upside down, and then finally set in the back of a delivery truck. The bear has no idea where he's going or what lies ahead; he only knows he is inside the box, outside of where he originally was, and now upside down, going who knows where. It doesn't take long until he falls off the truck inside, outside, and upside down in that wonderful box!

Most of us can probably relate to the bear; we like the security of a "box." It's predictable, safe, and, for the most part, a comfortable routine. However, it only stays that way until something comes around and turns it upside down. Then we find ourselves sent on an unplanned, unpredictable adventure we didn't sign up for. Life is often like that. It's full of events, surprises, and things you can't always plan for. Do we get disappointed? Sure, we do. We can even find ourselves feeling lost and, at times, desperate. We don't always know what to do. We feel upside down and unsure of what's coming next. This feeling of being unsure is okay; we need to understand that there is always more to the story than we see in these moments.

Jesus is our "box buster." Too often we can hide behind our "safe theology" and our "neatly" organized beliefs, but when life comes around and turns things upside down, we find ourselves not knowing what to do. Life was never meant to be lived in the confines of a box; there is no "perfect" theology (other than the person of Jesus), and life is a journey of learning and growing. We can, at times, find ourselves like the young bear in *Inside, Outside, Upside Down*. It's not something God does to set us back but to frame the next chapter in our life experiences.

Faith is for times like this. We need to learn to adjust, reset, and get rid of unnecessary things. We need to forge through the uncertainties so our lives and experiences can be reshaped into the design God intended for them. Most often, it's in those "inside, outside, upside down" moments that new things in us are birthed. Understanding becomes clearer, and what we thought to be our doom becomes a new opportunity. Through my own topsy-turvy adventures, I have learned there are many discoveries to be found in the unlikely places life often takes us.

POWER THOUGHT:

There are many discoveries to be found in the most unlikely places.

PERSONAL REFLECTION: What are you most likely afraid of when you enter the unfamiliar territory life's unpredictable situations can bring your way?

Day 31

GOD WITH (US)

Have you ever found yourself wondering where something is, when you're staring directly at that exact thing? Maybe you're not like me, but I find myself doing that more often than not (and it has nothing to do with age). You get so zeroed in, intensely focused on what you think you should be seeing, yet there it is, right before your eyes, and you can't see it. This is the same thing we often do with God's presence.

We can know God is real and experience His realness on so many levels, and we can even understand and believe that He never leaves us, yet many times we find ourselves in the midst of circumstances that are less than desirable. We become wound up, worked up, stretched thin, and stressed out. We feel completely alone in these situations and wonder where God is. We are so focused on what we think we should be focused on, that we fail to see that God is right there with us.

God is with us just like He was there with David as he stood up against Goliath. God was there with Shadrach, Meshach, and Abednego when they found themselves in so many impossible situations, thinking, *What do we do now?* God was there when Daniel was thrown into a pit and faced certain death. God was there when the nation of Israel faced insurmountable odds. Just like He was with them, God is in our lives, too—we just don't always recognize Him.

I have learned that just because we don't see God in a situation, doesn't mean He isn't there. God with us is a foundational reality we can always count on. The amazing part of all this? He isn't with us because we've done everything right, or because we have finally impressed Him enough, prayed the right kind of prayer, or know enough verses from the Good Book. His presence has nothing to do with that; rather, it has everything to do with who He (Jesus) is. I grew up in a church culture that taught that our relationship with God was mostly based on performance—my performance, to be exact. Wow, is that ever a tiring way to look at it, and the furthest thing from the truth. God never depends on our performance; instead, we are invited to depend solely upon His.

Life won't always be easy; we will be up against tough situations, but He will *always* be with us! His very name, Emmanuel, highlights this truth. Jesus is there through thick and thin, whether we feel it or not. So let's start looking at the situation we're in, and the circumstances that often surround us, differently. Instead of wondering where God is, let's start looking for Him in the middle of it all. Changing our perspective and focus will change everything!

POWER THOUGHT:

Don't get so zeroed in that you don't see what's right in front of you.

PERSONAL REFLECTION: What does "God With Us" mean to you in the everyday circumstances of life?

About the Author

Geoff Thiessen is a Jesus-loving pastor at the helm of a culture shift. He loves guns, bodybuilding, tattoos, and riding his Harley, and his life motto is, "Change your perspective, change your life." Geoff and his wife, Helen, both have a heart for people and a desire for REAL people to encounter REAL faith. With over 17 years of pastoral experience, Geoff has become a respected and gifted leader. He has a passion to see people discover who they are, and live their life to the fullest; he brings a fresh hope to everyday life. Geoff inspires people to see their value and shows how the Bible, and relationship with Jesus, isn't a system nor a religion, but is an empowering and ongoing, life-changing experience.